First Facts®

Whales and Dolphins Up Close

HUMPBACK WHALES UP CLOSE

by Jody Sullivan Rake

Consultant:
Deborah Nuzzolo
Education Manager
SeaWorld, San Diego

Capstone
press®
Mankato, Minnesota

First Facts is published by Capstone Press,
151 Good Counsel Drive, P.O. Box 669, Mankato, Minnesota 56002.
www.capstonepress.com

Books published by Capstone Press are manufactured with paper
containing at least 10 percent post-consumer waste.

Library of Congress Cataloging-in-Publication Data
Rake, Jody Sullivan.
    Humpback whales up close / by Jody Sullivan Rake.
    p. cm. — (First facts. Whales and dolphins up close)
    Includes bibliographical references and index.
    Summary: "Presents an up-close look at humpback whales, including their body
features, habitat, and life cycle" — Provided by publisher.
    ISBN 978-1-4296-3337-6 (library binding : alk. paper)
    1. Humpback whale — Juvenile literature. I. Title. II. Series.
QL737.C424R36 2010
599.5'25 — dc22   2009006004

Editorial Credits
Megan Schoeneberger, editor; Renée T. Doyle, set designer; Alison Thiele, book
    designer; Wanda Winch, media researcher

Photo Credits
Alamy/ArteSub, 19 (right)
Ardea/Francois Gohier, 11
Getty Images Inc./The Image Bank/Sue Flood, 13
Minden Pictures/Mitsuaki Iwago, 20
SeaPics.com/Amos Nachoum, 8; James D. Watt, 15, 21; Masa Ushioda, 1, 17
Shutterstock/Marilyn Volan, 2–3, 24
www.marinethemes.com/Kelvin Aitken, cover, 5, 6 (both), 8 (inset), 11 (inset), 18–19

TABLE OF CONTENTS

Giant but Graceful

A giant humpback whale leaps into the air. With a mighty splash, the huge **mammal** comes down in the water.

Humpbacks are some of the largest whales. They can be 40 to 50 feet (12 to 15 meters) long. That is about the length of a semitruck. Humpbacks weigh up to 80,000 pounds (36,300 kilograms).

mammal — a warm-blooded animal that has a backbone

dorsal fin

flipper ⟶

Flippers, Flukes, and Fins

Humpbacks use their flippers and **flukes** to swim. They pump their flukes up and down. Their long flippers help steer through the water.

Humpbacks' **dorsal fins** usually have a hump. Scientists can identify individual whales by the shape of their dorsal fins.

fluke

fluke — the wide, flat area at the end of a whale's tail

dorsal fin — the fin that sticks up from the middle of a whale's back

baleen

Blowholes

Humpback whales have two blowholes.
Humpbacks' blowholes are like human
nostrils, except they are on top of their heads.
They use their blowholes to breathe.

blowholes

Mighty Mouthfuls

Humpback whales are **baleen** whales. They don't have teeth. Instead, they use baleen to eat. Baleen hangs down from their upper jaw. It is stiff and hairy like a mustache.

baleen — long, fringed plates in the mouths of some whales

Hungry Humpbacks

Humpbacks are big, but their prey is tiny. These whales eat many kinds of small fish. But **krill** makes up most of their meals.

Baleen works like a strainer to filter krill out of the water. Humpback whales gulp huge mouthfuls of water. The baleen traps the krill, and the whale swallows its meal whole.

krill — a small, shrimplike animal

krill

Around the World

Humpbacks live in all the world's oceans. They spend summers in cold polar seas. Under their skin, a layer of fat called blubber keeps them warm.

Humpback Whale Range

Where humpback whales swim

North America

Europe

Asia

Africa

South America

Australia

N
W · E
S

Antarctica

Before winter, humpbacks **migrate** to warmer waters near the equator. Many humpbacks spend winters near Hawaii.

migrate — to move from one place to another

Life Cycle

Humpbacks are old enough to mate when they are 6 to 10 years old. Male and female humpbacks mate in early winter. One year later, female whales give birth to one calf.

Life Cycle of a Humpback Whale

Calf
Baby humpbacks are about 10 to 15 feet (3 to 4.6 meters) long.

Mom and Baby

Young
Humpbacks keep growing until they are 10 years old.

Adult
Humpbacks live to be 30 to 40 years old.

15

Humpback Calves

Humpback whale calves weigh up to 2,000 pounds (907 kilograms) at birth. Mothers and calves stay close together. They touch and rub each other often.

Calves drink milk from their mothers. They drink up to 130 gallons (492 liters) each day. The thick, rich milk helps them grow quickly.

Whale Songs

Male humpbacks sing. They squeeze air sacs near their blowholes. Air moves between the sacs. The moving air makes sounds. The sounds range from low, rumbling moans to squeaky squeals.

A whale often sings the same song for 20 minutes. Whales that live near each other sing the same songs.

Acrobats

Most big whales are not very active. But humpbacks are! They often breach, or leap into the air. They wave their flippers and slap them on the water. When they dive, their tail bursts out of the water.

fluke

Humpback whales team up to catch prey. Groups of humpbacks swim below a school of fish. The whales blow bubbles from their blowholes to confuse the fish. Then the whales swim up and gulp down the mixed-up prey!

Humpback Whales and People

Whalers hunted humpbacks during the 1800s. By the 1970s, only about 1,000 humpbacks were left. Now laws protect humpback whales. Whalers are allowed to hunt only a few humpbacks each year. The whales' numbers have grown to about 10,000.

Glossary

baleen (BAY-leen) — long, fringed plates in the mouths of some whales

blubber (BLUH-buhr) — a layer of fat under a whale's skin that protects the whale from the cold

breach (BREECH) — to jump out of the water

dorsal fin (DOR-suhl FIN) — the fin that sticks up from the middle of a whale's back

fluke (FLOOK) — the wide, flat area at the end of a whale's tail; whales move their flukes to swim.

krill (KRIL) — a small, shrimplike animal

mammal (MAM-uhl) — a warm–blooded animal that breathes air; mammals have hair or fur; female mammals feed milk to their young.

migrate (MYE-grate) — to move from one place to another

Read More

Hardyman, Robyn. *Whales.* The World of Animals. Redding, Conn.: Brown Bear Books, 2009.

Nicklin, Flip, and Linda Nicklin. *Face to Face with Whales.* Face to Face with Animals. Washington, D.C.: National Geographic, 2008.

Stille, Darlene R. *I Am a Whale: The Life of a Humpback Whale.* I Live in the Ocean. Minneapolis: Picture Window Books, 2005.

Internet Sites

FactHound offers a safe, fun way to find Internet sites related to this book. All of the sites on FactHound have been researched by our staff.

Here's all you do:

Visit *www.facthound.com*

FactHound will fetch the best sites for you!

Index